Original title:
A Whisper of Snow

Copyright © 2024 Swan Charm
All rights reserved.

Author: Linda Leevike
ISBN HARDBACK: 978-9916-79-816-4
ISBN PAPERBACK: 978-9916-79-817-1
ISBN EBOOK: 978-9916-79-818-8

Soft Hues of Winter's Canvas

Gentle whispers of cold air,
Lace upon the frozen ground.
Colors pale in dawn's soft light,
Nature's brush strokes all around.

Silent flurries dance and sway,
Kissing branches, bare and still.
Quiet moments softly play,
In the calm, it's time to chill.

Crystal crystals, pure and bright,
Blanket fields in tranquil grace.
Shadows stretch with fading light,
Resting in this winter space.

Echoes of the world asleep,
Dreams wrapped in a frosty shroud.
Winter secrets softly keep,
Beneath the heavens, proud.

In this season, breath like smoke,
Fragrant pine and cinnamon.
Nature sings a gentle cloak,
As winter's dance has just begun.

A Symphony of White Dreams

Drifting softly through the trees,
Snowflakes twirl like dancers bright.
Whispers carried by the breeze,
In a world of purest white.

Gentle hush the night bestows,
Stars a-glimmer, silver sheen.
Every heart in winter knows,
Magic woven, calm and keen.

Frosted breath in chilly air,
Memories wrapped in layers deep.
Frozen moments linger there,
As the world begins to sleep.

Icicles like crystal spears,
Hanging from the rooftops high.
Silent songs that winter cheers,
Underneath the slate gray sky.

In the quiet, dreams take flight,
Whirling softly, chasing light.
A symphony of white, it seams,
We find peace in winter's dreams.

Serene Beauty of the Snowfall

Snowflakes dance down from the sky,
A blanket of white, soft and shy.
Whispers of winter in the air,
Nature's embrace, delicate and rare.

Branches adorned with shimmering lace,
Tranquility wrapped in winter's grace.
Footprints vanish, time stands still,
In the hush of snow, we find our thrill.

Glistening crystals catch the light,
Sparkling dreams in the silent night.
Each flake unique, a fleeting art,
Serenity whispers, it warms the heart.

Snowbound Recollections

Memories drift like snow on the breeze,
Frosty mornings bring nostalgia with ease.
Laughter echoes from childhood days,
In snowbound wonder, life gently sways.

The soft crunch beneath our boots,
Sleds racing down the hills, absolute hoots.
Warm fires crackle with stories untold,
In the heart of winter, memories unfold.

Frosty windows frame our dreams,
Hot cocoa swirls in warm, cozy beams.
Family together, wrapped in love,
Snowbound joy, a blessing from above.

The Gentle Chill of Solitude

Stillness envelops the world outside,
A gentle chill where thoughts can reside.
In solitude's arms, we find our peace,
Winter's embrace allows for a release.

Snow blankets whispers of the night,
A quiet retreat, soft and bright.
Moments linger, time loses pace,
In the cool air, we find our place.

Stars twinkle softly through the frost,
In solitude's beauty, we are not lost.
In the silence, dreams take flight,
The gentle chill wraps us tight.

Ephemeral Whispers

A delicate touch, the snowflakes fall,
Ephemeral whispers, a soft, sweet call.
Each flake a story, unique and rare,
Fleeting moments we're lucky to share.

As twilight glows in shades of blue,
Nature's canvas, a wondrous view.
In the stillness, our hearts align,
With the beauty of snow, so divine.

Time fades gently, like melting snow,
Life's precious secrets in soft winds blow.
Catch them in laughter, let them flow,
In ephemeral whispers, we learn to grow.

Hushed Elegance

In the quiet of the night,
Moonlight casts its grace,
Softly draping shadows,
In a tranquil embrace.

Whispers of the breeze,
Serenade the stillness,
Every leaf a dancer,
Nature's quiet thrillness.

Stars twinkle above,
In a velvet sky,
Each a distant story,
As moments flutter by.

A world draped in calm,
Where time gently flows,
Beauty in the silence,
Where serenity grows.

Hushed elegance surrounds,
In the still of the night,
A melody of peace,
Bathed in soft moonlight.

The Gentle Fall of White

Softly whispers the air,
As snow begins to dance,
Each flake a fleeting thought,
In a delicate trance.

Blankets cover the earth,
Wrapping all in white,
A peaceful transformation,
In the hush of night.

Trees wear coats of silver,
Branches bowed in grace,
Nature holds its breath,
In this tranquil space.

Children's laughter echoes,
Through the frosty gleam,
Creating memories,
In a snowy dream.

The gentle fall of white,
Cradles all in peace,
A moment's sweet embrace,
Where all worries cease.

Secrets of the Shimmering Drift

In the depth of twilight,
Stars begin to glow,
Whispers of the cosmos,
In a celestial flow.

Drifting through the night,
Moonlight paints the ground,
Each ray a hidden secret,
In silence profound.

Waves of shimmering light,
Kiss the frozen lake,
Where dreams and shadows stir,
In ripples they make.

The universe in awe,
Unveils its mystic art,
Each flicker, a reminder,
Of the beauty of the heart.

Secrets softly shimmer,
Underneath the stars,
In the dance of night's veil,
Our journey is ours.

Frosted Whispers

In the morning light,
Frost begins to gleam,
Nature's softest whispers,
In a crystal dream.

Each blade dressed in diamonds,
As the sun takes flight,
A chorus of the chilly,
In the dawn's delight.

The world seems to sparkle,
With every step we take,
Frosted whispers linger,
In the paths we make.

Breath hangs in the air,
A cloud of gentle mist,
Nature's art awakens,
In the calm, we exist.

Frosted whispers call,
As the day unfolds,
In the beauty of the chill,
A warmth that the heart holds.

Sketches in the Icy Air

Frosty drawings grace the sky,
Whispers of the night pass by.
Crystals dance in silver light,
A canvas bright, a stunning sight.

Silent breezes softly weave,
Tales of winter, hearts believe.
Beneath the stars, the shadows play,
In the chill, dreams drift away.

Footprints mark the path we tread,
Stories in the snow, unsaid.
Glimmers fall, like secrets there,
Sketches form in the icy air.

Branches twinkle, branches sway,
Nature's art, in pure display.
Each breath clouds in the night's embrace,
A fleeting moment, time and space.

As dawn breaks, colors bloom,
Awakening after winter's gloom.
With every hue, life's stories flare,
In the beauty of the icy air.

Whispers of the Frozen Ground

Beneath the layer, quiet lies,
All the dreams the earth supplies.
Gentle murmurs, secrets speak,
In the stillness, wisdom seeks.

Frosted grass with glistening dew,
Nature's whispers, soft and true.
Hidden life beneath the white,
Tales of wonder, pure delight.

Every snowflake tells a tale,
Of the wild that will prevail.
Underneath the surface rests,
Memories wrapped in nature's best.

Echoes linger in the cold,
Winter's stories to be told.
In the silence, hearts will find,
Links to seasons intertwined.

As the winter sun ascends,
Whispers change, the cycle bends.
Life will rise from frozen ground,
In the quiet, peace is found.

Secrets in the Snowdrifts

Silent valleys wrapped in white,
Snowdrifts hold secrets, out of sight.
Nature's treasures, subtle, deep,
In the cold, old stories sleep.

Layered whispers in the chill,
Every drift a silent thrill.
Footprints lead to unknown ways,
Where the winter magic stays.

Beneath the frost, warmth remains,
Hidden truths in winter's veins.
Branches bow with loaded tales,
In the hush, the spirit sails.

As shadows stretch and new day wakes,
Life ascends with every flake.
All the treasures time has sown,
In the snowdrifts, we're not alone.

In the stillness of the night,
Secrets shimmer, bold and bright.
Through the silence, hearts can know,
The embrace of winter's glow.

Echoes of Winter's Kiss

Winter wraps the world in lace,
A tender touch, a soft embrace.
Cold winds carry echoes clear,
Of the beauty that draws near.

Silent moments, crisp and bright,
In the stillness, pure delight.
Nature hums a soothing tune,
Underneath the silver moon.

Each breath fogs the biting air,
Whispers float, a timeless prayer.
In the chill, the hearts align,
Frosty breath, a sacred sign.

A touch of white upon the earth,
Each flake brings a moment's worth.
Captured in this frozen bliss,
All is found in winter's kiss.

As twilight dances, stars ignite,
Guiding us through the velvet night.
In their glow, we find our bliss,
Echoes linger of winter's kiss.

Dreaming with Flurries

Snowflakes dance like whispers,
In a gentle, rolling breeze.
Wishing dreams take flight,
In a world of silent ease.

Each flurry writes a story,
Upon the canvas white.
Laughter fades in soft embrace,
As day yields to night.

Underneath the silver glow,
The stars begin to peep.
I drift through frosty realms,
In a night so calm, so deep.

The air is crisp with wonder,
As visions swirl and twirl.
In dreams of winter magic,
I let my heart unfurl.

With every soft landing,
I hold the warmth inside.
Dreaming with flurries fleeting,
A cozy, peaceful ride.

Frosty Veils of Silence

A hush blankets the forest,
In the arms of winter's chill.
Frosty veils softly cover,
Every tree and every hill.

The world pauses in wonder,
As snowflakes twirl and twine.
Nature holds its breath in awe,
In this moment, divine.

Crystal glimmers greet the morning,
As sunlight starts to break.
A symphony of silence sings,
While shadows softly wake.

Footsteps crunch in slow rhythm,
Leaving trails of fleeting grace.
In frosty veils of silence,
I find a warm embrace.

To wander in this stillness,
Is to cherish every breath.
In nature's quiet beauty,
I feel the stillness of death.

Winter's Undisturbed Poetry

In the heart of winter's quiet,
Verses linger in the snow.
Words are written with the frost,
In a world that's soft and slow.

Every branch holds a secret,
Every shadow tells a tale.
Winter's undisturbed poetry,
Is whispered on the gale.

Nature composes softly,
With the wind's gentle sighs.
A chorus of frozen beauty,
Underneath the vast, gray skies.

As twilight wraps the landscape,
In a warm and tender glow.
I hear the echo of the night,
In the silence, soft and low.

These words, though cold and fleeting,
Live in hearts that choose to hear.
Winter's song, forever cherished,
Is the music of the year.

Tranquility of a Frosted Landscape

In the stillness of the morning,
Frost adorns the slumbering ground.
Tranquility envelops all,
In a world that feels profound.

The trees wear coats of crystal,
As sunlight peeks through haze.
A tranquil, frosted landscape,
Font of peace and lazy days.

Every breath draws in the magic,
As nature whispers low.
I am caught in moments treasured,
In a soft, enchanting glow.

Wandering through this splendor,
Time drifts on like smoke.
Each step a gentle heartbeat,
In a dream that we invoke.

With frozen streams reflecting,
The beauty that I see.
In a tranquil, frosted landscape,
I find serenity.

In the Stillness of Winter

The world is draped in white,
Silence blankets the night.
Stars twinkle with frosty glow,
In the stillness, dreams flow.

Breath clouds in the cool air,
Nature's peace beyond compare.
Footsteps muffled in the snow,
Whispers of winter, soft and slow.

Trees wear coats made of ice,
Each branch a crystal slice.
Time seems to gently pause,
In this season's quiet cause.

Moonlight dances on the frost,
In this serenity, none are lost.
Hearts find warmth in shared embrace,
In the stillness, we find grace.

Memories wrapped in cold,
Winter tales waiting to be told.
To every soul, a gentle call,
In the stillness, we share all.

Chilled Memories

Winds of the past softly sigh,
As memories drift and fly.
Frozen laughter in the air,
Chilled echoes everywhere.

Footprints traced on snowy ground,
In quiet spaces, peace is found.
Each moment frozen in time,
Captured in winter's rhyme.

Crimson sunsets, fading light,
Golden dreams take flight at night.
Frosted glass, secrets to share,
In the chill, we find our care.

Silent woods, a gentle hush,
As heartbeats quiet in the rush.
Beneath the snow, life waits anew,
Chilled memories, soft and true.

Gathered warmth by fireside glow,
Tales of winter's ebb and flow.
In every breath, a story bleeds,
Chilled memories, as time proceeds.

The Quiet of Falling Snow

Snowflakes dance from sky to ground,
In each drift, peace is found.
Whispers of white grace the air,
The quiet of falling, soft and rare.

Nature holds its breath in wait,
As silence weaves a silver fate.
Branches sigh with a gentle bend,
In this stillness, hearts can mend.

Footfalls in the muted white,
Separate shadows in the night.
Every flake a dream untold,
In the quiet, warmth unfolds.

Stars emerge in the evening's glow,
Filling the world with silver show.
Time suspends in the winter's embrace,
In the quiet, we find our place.

With every drift, a story begins,
In the stillness, the world spins.
Together, we dream and roam,
The quiet of falling snow, our home.

Frosted Memories

Morning breaks with icy light,
Frosted whispers, pure and bright.
Each breath a cloud, a fleeting sign,
In winter's clutch, we intertwine.

Laughter echoing in the chill,
Time stands still; we feel the thrill.
Past moments linger, like the frost,
In memories held, nothing's lost.

Softly falling, a quiet grace,
Life's tapestry, each thread a trace.
Frosted visions gently gleam,
In winter's hold, we share a dream.

Candles flicker, shadows sway,
In warmed rooms where stories play.
Time may freeze, but hearts remain,
Frosted memories, sweet refrain.

Through the window, views unfold,
December's magic, a tale retold.
Embrace the chill, let warmth arise,
Frosted memories never die.

Echoes in the Frost

Crystals glimmer in the light,
Whispers caught in chilly air.
Each step leaves a sound so slight,
Nature holds its breath to stare.

Beneath the trees, shadows creep,
Silent stories left untold.
Footprints vanish, dreams we keep,
Worn by time, and growing old.

A pale sun dips, the day grows cold,
Each horizon, a canvas bare.
Echoes linger, life unfolds,
In the stillness, we must care.

Memories etched in white and grey,
Soft reminders of what we've lost.
In the frost, we find our way,
Seeking warmth, no matter the cost.

As night descends, the stars align,
Twinkling tales of endless hope.
In the darkness, hearts entwine,
Winter's beauty helps us cope.

Dance of the Snowflakes

Spirals falling from the sky,
Each flake tells a tale in flight.
In their dance, the world sighs,
Softly kissing all with white.

Twirls and twists in frosty air,
Nature's waltz, a gentle grace.
Moments fleeting, nothing spare,
In this ballet, we find our place.

Children laugh, arms open wide,
Chasing dreams in winter's arms.
Snowflakes swirl, a joyful tide,
Capturing all of nature's charms.

Settling down on roofs and trees,
A blanket wrapped around the earth.
Whispers carried on the breeze,
In their beauty, we find mirth.

As the sun begins to set,
Glistening diamonds in a row.
In this moment, hearts are met,
Lost in the dance, forever flow.

Silence in a Snowfall

Gentle whispers on the ground,
Covering all in soft embrace.
Perfect stillness all around,
Time suspended, slows its pace.

Pine trees draped in winter's glow,
Notes of silence fill the air.
In this moment, peace will flow,
Sorrow mingles with the fair.

Softly falling, dreams take flight,
Hushed beneath a snowy shroud.
In the heart of winter's night,
Silent prayers rise from the crowd.

Each flake a thought, unique, profound,
Gathering, merging, forming whole.
In stillness, answers can be found,
A winter's night heals every soul.

As dawn breaks with a tender light,
A world reborn, fresh and new.
Silence dances into sight,
In the snowfall, we renew.

The Invisibility of Winter's Touch

Mystery cloaked in pale white,
Shadows stretch across the ground.
Winter's breath, a secret rite,
Where echoes of the past resound.

Frosty tendrils lace the trees,
Caressing bark with gentle care.
In this chill, the heart finds ease,
Magic woven everywhere.

A light whisper, a fleeting kiss,
Blankets nature in its arms.
Invisibility like bliss,
Transforming landscapes with its charms.

Moments captured, flurries freeze,
Memories forged in frigid time.
Winter's touch, an artist's tease,
Crafting beauty, pure and prime.

As we walk through quiet streets,
In this splendor, we can see.
The invisibility of feats,
Winter's touch, a sanctuary.

Midnight's Silent Blanket

The moon whispers softly bright,
Wrapping the world in gentle light.
Stars glitter in the velvet sky,
As night unfolds its lullaby.

A blanket of silence, deep and wide,
Cuddling the earth with calm inside.
Winds carry secrets, hushed and low,
In the dark, where dreams freely flow.

Trees stand tall, shadows extend,
Nature's calm, a tranquil blend.
With every heartbeat, the stillness grows,
In the arms of night, the soul knows.

Footsteps muffled on the lane,
Echoes of whispers, memories remain.
Under the stars, the heart takes flight,
In midnight's embrace, all feels right.

Time stands still, the world is at peace,
In this moment, worries cease.
Midnight's blanket, a soothing touch,
Reminding us, we are loved so much.

Starlit Snowflakes

Falling softly, a dance of white,
Starlit snowflakes glimmer in the night.
Whirling gently, they twirl and wane,
Covering the earth like a silvery chain.

Each flake is a whisper from above,
A delicate gift, a token of love.
As they land, they hug the ground,
In their embrace, peace is found.

Children laugh, their joy takes flight,
Building dreams in the winter light.
Snowmen rising, frost-filled cheer,
In starlit moments, magic is near.

The world transforms with each falling piece,
In layers of wonder, worries release.
As night drapes its cloak, the snowflakes gleam,
In their soft glow, we dare to dream.

Underneath the starlit glow,
Nature whispers secrets in the snow.
Each snowflake unique, a story they weave,
In the shimmering chill, we believe.

The Caress of Crystal Landscapes

Frosted branches, a sight so rare,
Crystal landscapes beyond compare.
Nature's artistry, a winter's grace,
Every corner a new embrace.

Icicles shimmer in morning light,
A silent symphony, pure delight.
Fields wear a gown of silvery hue,
In every breath, the magic renews.

Whispers of breezes, gently play,
As shadows dance, the sun's first ray.
A tapestry woven from ice and snow,
In this world, tranquility flows.

In the stillness, the heart can roam,
Finding solace, a sense of home.
Crystal landscapes call us near,
In their beauty, the world feels clear.

Every step on this frozen ground,
Echoes softly, a soothing sound.
In nature's arms, our spirits rise,
Under the vast, open skies.

Soft Shadows on the Ground

Evening settles with a gentle sigh,
Soft shadows stretch beneath the sky.
As daylight fades, the world transforms,
In twilight's cloak, new magic warms.

Whispers of night begin to play,
Guiding the stars to find their way.
Each soft shadow tells a tale,
Of day's embrace and night's unveil.

Beneath the trees, where secrets lie,
Moonbeams trickle, a silvery sigh.
In hushed tones, the night reveals,
The beauty in what stillness feels.

Soft footsteps dance on the ground,
Wings of night creatures lightly sound.
A lullaby sung by leaves and air,
In the dusk, we breathe in care.

So embrace the shadows, soft and deep,
In their comfort, the world will sleep.
Soft shadows whisper, hearts confound,
In the quiet night, solace is found.

The Musical Hush of White

Blankets of snow cover the ground,
Silence wraps the world around,
Soft footsteps in the quiet night,
Whispers of frost, pure and white.

Trees shimmer in a ghostly glow,
Crystalline beauty starts to show,
Underneath a moon's soft kiss,
Winter's song, a breath of bliss.

Icicles dangle, sharp and clear,
Nature's art, so stark, so near,
With every flake, a story spun,
A tranquil scene where night has won.

In this hush, the heart finds peace,
All worries fade, they gently cease,
A moment paused in time's embrace,
The world adorned in winter's lace.

Within this calm, a melody stirs,
Soft notes that speak, like whispered furs,
In the shadowed trees, a quiet choir,
Of dreams that dance around the fire.

Whispers on the Frosted Path

Footsteps crunch on the frosty trail,
Secrets ride the winter's gale,
Each whisper echoes in the night,
Carried forth in silver light.

Pine trees sway, their boughs adorned,
With icy jewels, subtly worn,
Every sound, a gentle sigh,
As winter's breath drifts softly by.

Stars flicker in the cobalt skies,
Twinkling gems, the world complies,
The moon, a lantern, guiding fate,
On this path where dreams await.

Frosted air, a taste so pure,
Each moment held, and hearts endure,
A journey cloaked in icy hues,
Wrapped in nature's tranquil muse.

With every step, the world unfolds,
Stories of old, in whispers told,
Upon this path, souls intertwine,
Underneath the starlit line.

Glacial Dreams

In the realm where ice does gleam,
Fragments of a frozen dream,
Shadows dance on the glacial blue,
Whispers of life that once we knew.

Mountains stand with jagged grace,
Guardians of this endless space,
In their embrace, the silence swells,
Mysteries that the cold dispels.

A vision glides on the icy stream,
Reflections caught in winter's beam,
Where time feels still, and hope takes flight,
In glacial dreams, all is right.

Hushed moments linger, spirits soar,
As glacial wonders beckon more,
Each breath a gift in the air so rare,
A symphony of frost to share.

In this realm of quiet sighs,
Nature's canvas fills the skies,
With every glance, the heart is filled,
By glacial dreams that time has willed.

Echoes on the Winter Breeze

Echoes dance on the winter breeze,
Soft as snow that falls from trees,
A haunting song of the night's refrain,
Carried forth by the gentle rain.

The world is wrapped in a cozy shroud,
Whispers linger, soft and proud,
A tapestry of frost unfurls,
In these moments, magic swirls.

Moonlight bathes the frozen ground,
In a silver glow, peace is found,
Each breath, a cloud that drifts away,
In winter's arms, we long to stay.

Stars twinkle like distant dreams,
Painting tales in subtle beams,
With every gust, a story shared,
In the chill, we feel prepared.

In echoes soft, our hearts align,
Through winter's kiss, life's grand design,
With every whisper on the air,
We find ourselves, all that we share.

Crystal Delicacies

In the garden of frost, they glow bright,
Fragile wonders, a shimmering sight.
With a touch so gentle, they dance in the breeze,
Whispers of beauty, the heart they seize.

Softly they glisten, like stars in the night,
Wrapped in the silence, they capture delight.
Each petal a treasure, each flake a rare gem,
Nature's own canvas, a delicate stem.

Frost kisses the earth, a moment in time,
In the chill of the air, they create perfect rhyme.
In shadows, they linger, a breathless embrace,
Elusive and fleeting, they vanish with grace.

The Soft Touch of Ice

In twilight's calm, a veil of white,
Crystal soft, enchanting light.
Each flake a whisper, a secret untold,
Caressing the earth in a shimmer of gold.

Beneath the moon's gaze, they silently fall,
A blanket of dreams, a soothing call.
Gentle and tender, they wrap the night,
The world transformed, a serene delight.

Frost patterns twinkle on windowpanes,
Fragile artistry that lingers and gains.
Every breath curls in the frosty air,
A moment suspended, a gentle stare.

Shadows of the Falling Glisten

In twilight's embrace, shadows play,
Glistening softly, leading the way.
Each flake a dancer, each breath a sigh,
Together they weave where the silence lies.

The world hushes softly, a lullaby sweet,
With every step on this delicate sheet.
Twinkling reflections that shimmer and bend,
A canvas of winter where dreams never end.

With whispers of frost, the night unfolds,
A story of beauty that winter holds.
Shadows linger, kissed by the light,
In the heart of the frost, everything feels right.

Murmurs in a Snowy World

In a world draped in snow, whispers arise,
Murmurs of magic beneath starlit skies.
Footsteps crunch softly, a melody pure,
Echoes of silence that softly endure.

Each snowflake settles, a delicate dream,
In winter's soft grip, we find our theme.
Gentle lullabies carried on the breeze,
Transported to places where worries freeze.

The air filled with wonder, each breath a delight,
In the snowy embrace, hearts feel so light.
Together we wander, hand in hand tight,
In murmured moments, we wrap the night.

Winter's Gentle Breath

Winter whispers soft and low,
As the world begins to slow.
Frosted trees in quiet grace,
Nature's hush, a warm embrace.

Snowflakes dance on gentle air,
Each one perfect, none to spare.
Blanket white on silent ground,
In this peace, pure joy is found.

Heartbeats echo through the night,
Underneath the moon's soft light.
Stars twinkle high above the pines,
In this stillness, love entwines.

Candles flicker in the dark,
Fires glow with a cozy spark.
Hot cocoa warms our coldest hands,
Together here, the heart still stands.

With every breath, the chill retreats,
Winter's melody repeats.
The beauty found in quiet days,
Holds us captive in its ways.

Frosted Echoes

Frosted whispers in the dawn,
Nature's breath, a perfect song.
Icicles hang like crystal tears,
Silent stories of our fears.

Branches bear a heavy load,
Covered paths where silence flowed.
Footsteps crunching through the snow,
Each step leads to thoughts that grow.

A chill embraced beneath the cloud,
Softened by a stillness loud.
Winter's heart, so bold and bright,
Wraps us in its frosted light.

Through the windows, warmth invites,
As the world outside ignites.
Frosted patterns grace the glass,
Moments captured, hours pass.

Echoes linger from the night,
A tapestry of pure delight.
Memories made in the cold air,
Frosted whispers linger there.

Silent Shimmer

The world glows in quiet light,
Softly wrapped in winter's white.
Each star twinkles in the sky,
A silent shimmer drawing nigh.

Frozen streams hold secrets tight,
Crystals dance in the pale moonlight.
Whispers echo, clear and bright,
Nature's song, a pure delight.

In the woods, where shadows play,
Each moment holds a soft ballet.
Snowflakes twirl in wild delight,
Painting dreams in the hush of night.

Buried deep beneath the frost,
Lies the life that winter lost.
Yet in silence, hope takes flight,
Waiting for the sun's warm light.

Through the stillness, hearts converge,
As the spirit starts to surge.
Winter's charm a brief affair,
A silent shimmer, everywhere.

The Quiet Blanket

A quiet blanket, soft and wide,
Covers earth with a gentle pride.
In the stillness, dreams unfold,
Stories of the winter cold.

Hushed whispers fill the air,
Magic dances everywhere.
Frozen laughter, crisp and clear,
In this moment, time feels near.

Footprints trace a winding path,
Winding through the aftermath.
Every step a tale to tell,
In the quiet, all is well.

Breath of ice, a fleeting chill,
Wraps the world with peace, so still.
In the dark, soft shadows fall,
Nature's canvas, a silent call.

As the morning sun awakes,
Sparkling dew on glistening flakes.
A quiet blanket holds us tight,
Winter's wonder, pure delight.

Crystalline Murmurs

Whispers float on winter's breath,
Branches shimmer, silvered wreaths.
Nature's art, a silent hymn,
In the stillness, life's essence brim.

Gentle echoes weave through trees,
Softly swaying, carried with ease.
The world dons its frosty gown,
As night descends, secrets abound.

Moonlight dances on a lake,
Each ripple, a gentle shake.
Stars wink softly from above,
In this realm, I'm lost in love.

Footprints mark a fleeting trail,
In quietude, dreams unveil.
Crystalline murmurs call to me,
In their embrace, I am free.

Flurries of Serenity

Softly cascading, flakes descend,
A dance of grace, winter's friend.
Blanketing earth in purest white,
Transforming shadows into light.

Silence reigns, a gentle pause,
Nature breathes, as time withdraws.
With each flurry, worries cease,
Whispers of calm, a sweet release.

In the stillness, hearts align,
Touched by peace, a spark divine.
Footsteps crunch on pristine snow,
In this haven, spirits flow.

Every breath, a frosted sigh,
Beneath the vast and open sky.
Flurries swirl, a soft ballet,
In winter's arms, I long to stay.

A Dance of White Feathers

The world adorned in purest light,
Feathers drift, a wondrous sight.
Twisting, twirling, soft and slow,
Nature's waltz, a gentle flow.

Each flake whispers tales of old,
In their folds, warmth to behold.
Whirling round, like dreams set free,
In that dance, just you and me.

Textures blend, a canvas bright,
Shrouded in soft, dreamy white.
Together we embrace the chill,
Life's simple joys, we will fulfill.

As moments pass, we stand as one,
Chasing light, the day begun.
A dance of white, in crisp air clear,
In pure delight, we lose our fear.

Beneath the Icy Veil

Beneath a shroud of icy lace,
Nature slumbers, holds her grace.
Silent whispers, secrets shared,
In this stillness, hearts are bared.

Frozen rivers winding slow,
Reflecting dreams that softly glow.
Every branch a crystal crown,
In the silence, beauty's found.

Glimmering light on nature's skin,
Invites the warmth to dwell within.
Underneath, the earth will breathe,
Awakening life, as winters leave.

A world transformed, pure and bright,
With the dawn, dispelling night.
Beneath the icy veil, we wait,
For spring's embrace to celebrate.

Veils of Winter's Breath

The dawn breaks soft and white,
Veils of frost embrace the night.
Whispers dance in biting air,
Nature holds its breath with care.

Branches drape in icy lace,
Silent beauty speaks with grace.
Footsteps crunch on crystal ground,
In this hush, peace can be found.

A world wrapped in glistening dreams,
Frozen rivers, silver streams.
Time stands still, a fleeting sigh,
Underneath the slate-gray sky.

Each flake tells a tale of old,
Crystals painted, pure as gold.
Winter's breath, a cloak so fine,
In each moment, pure divine.

As shadows stretch the day away,
Stars emerge, in skies they play.
Wrapped in warmth, we find our peace,
Veils of winter gently cease.

Chilled Murmurs

Frosted whispers greet the dawn,
Chilled murmurs stretch upon the lawn.
Trees shake off the night's embrace,
Clarity in nature's grace.

Snowflakes drift on unseen trails,
Echoes of soft winter gales.
In the still, a promise lies,
Underneath the muted skies.

The world transformed, a canvas bright,
Timid shadows dance in light.
Frozen laughter fills the air,
Moments linger, free from care.

Beneath the stars, the silence gleams,
Echoes fade like distant dreams.
Every breath, a crystal spell,
In this winter's tranquil swell.

As daylight wanes, the moon ascends,
Chilled murmurs echo, never ends.
A symphony, soft and clear,
Winter's song, for all to hear.

The Quieting Flurries

Flurries spiral through the air,
Whirling softly without a care.
Each small dance, a fleeting glance,
Whispers weave in winter's trance.

Quiet blankets cloak the land,
Frosted whispers, gentle and grand.
A hush falls softly, time stands still,
As nature calms, it bends to will.

Lights flicker in the fading day,
Shadows murmur, softly sway.
In the stillness, hearts align,
Together wrapped, yours and mine.

Fallen flakes, with secrets shared,
In their essence, beauty bared.
A world anew, in muted tones,
Softly draped, in silence grown.

As twilight deepens, dreams take flight,
Through the flurries, pure delight.
In this quiet, moments gleam,
Lost in winter's tender dream.

Snowflakes' Softest Secrets

Snowflakes fall like whispered thoughts,
Softest secrets time begot.
In the silence, tales unfold,
Nature's warmth breaks winter's cold.

Each flake dances, twirls around,
Landing soft on sacred ground.
A gentle hush blankets the night,
In twilight's arms, all feels right.

Footprints vanish in the snow,
Silent stories, winds will blow.
Shimmering grace, a moment's cheer,
In these whispers, love draws near.

Chill embraces the evening's glow,
Mysteries cradle us below.
Fires crackle, hearts ignite,
As warmth touches the frosty night.

With each flake, a soft decree,
Whispers of what's yet to be.
In winter's hold, we find repose,
Secrets shared, like wind that blows.

Ghostly Patterns on the Ground

In shadows deep, the secrets lie,
Forgotten tales of days gone by.
A faint trace left from steps above,
Whispers of earth, a forgotten love.

The wind awakens ancient dreams,
Painting stories with silent screams.
Fleeting moments etched in time,
Ghostly patterns, a fleeting rhyme.

Among the leaves, the past does dance,
In every rustle, a haunting glance.
Echoes linger, soft as night,
Ghostly patterns, a solemn sight.

A tapestry woven with nature's hand,
Glimmers of hope in a shadowed land.
Each imprint speaks of journeys bold,
In the chill, these stories unfold.

Beneath the moon, the silence sighs,
As time drifts softly, the past replies.
In every corner, the ghosts remain,
Patterns on ground, a spectral chain.

Treading Lightly in Snow

Soft as whispers, footsteps fall,
Each crunch a note in winter's call.
The world adorned in purest white,
Draped in magic, a tranquil sight.

Gentle flakes dance, twirl, and glide,
Cover the earth, a serene tide.
In the stillness, secrets keep,
Where nature's blanket lulls to sleep.

With each breath, the frost does bite,
Yet heartbeats warm against the night.
A trace of joy where memories flow,
Life's sweet embrace in falling snow.

Wander where the shadows glide,
Footprints fade as dreams collide.
Treading lightly, spirits soar,
In this white realm, we ask for more.

As twilight falls, the silence reigns,
Echoes of laughter, soft refrains.
In winter's grasp, we find our peace,
Treading lightly, our worries cease.

An Embrace of Crystal

Beneath the frost, the world does gleam,
In fragile beauty, a silken dream.
Crystals dangle from every branch,
Nature's art in a silent dance.

Sunlight catches, a radiant show,
Reflecting whispers of fresh fall snow.
Each sparkle tells of winter's breath,
An embrace soft as a gentle death.

Amidst the trees, the light entwines,
Shimmering notes penned through the pines.
In icy chambers, secrets near,
An embrace of crystal, crystal clear.

As twilight paints the skies with grace,
The diamond glimmer finds its place.
With every shadow, a story's told,
In frozen arms, a beauty bold.

So let the chill caress your skin,
In winter's grace, let life begin.
Hold tight the warmth that love imparts,
In an embrace of crystal hearts.

Winter's Whispering Breath

A gentle sigh between the trees,
Winter's breath, a soft reprieve.
In every flake that drifts and sways,
   Nature's song in muted grays.

Hushed is the world as night descends,
With whispered secrets, the winter bends.
   Stars above in blankets bright,
   Guide the dreams into the night.

The icy wind, a fleeting kiss,
In frosted air, we find our bliss.
Echoing through the silent land,
Winter's whisper, a guiding hand.

Embraced by chill, we pause and listen,
   To stories told as shadows glisten.
   In every breath, the chill we feel,
Winter's breath, both harsh and real.

A call of magic drifts on high,
   As starlit wonders swirl and fly.
In every heartbeat, the cold we share,
Winter's whispering breath fills the air.

Midnight's Frosted Lace

Underneath the silver sky,
Whispers of the night breeze sigh.
Frosted lace on slumbering trees,
Nature's beauty, quiet, and free.

Stars twinkle as they softly gleam,
In the stillness, shadows dream.
Moonlight dances, casting charms,
Embracing Earth in its arms.

Crickets chirp a soft goodbye,
As hushed wings of owls glide by.
Every breath a misty trace,
A world adorned in frosted lace.

Footprints echo, lost and found,
In this silent, sacred ground.
Each flake tells a story old,
A magic realm, a sight to behold.

Morning light begins to rise,
Warming hues replace the skies.
Yet in memory, forever stays,
The beauty of midnight's frosted lace.

The Softest Touch of Winter

Gentle snowflakes fall like dreams,
Whispering secrets in the beams.
Blanketing the world in white,
A soft touch through the quiet night.

Branches bow with frosted crowns,
Tranquil beauty in sleepy towns.
Each corner glimmers, pure and bright,
As winter casts its gentle light.

Children laugh and play outside,
In snowy realms, their joy can't hide.
Building castles, snowmen tall,
In wonderland, they dance and sprawl.

Hot cocoa warms their tiny hands,
While stories shared in cozy lands.
Crackling fires, a warm embrace,
Reflecting on the winter's grace.

As daylight fades, the stars ignite,
Promising magic through the night.
Embracing all in soft embrace,
The softest touch of winter's grace.

Frozen Dreams Unfurled

In a world of icy streams,
Whispers carry frozen dreams.
Each crystal shard a wish set free,
In the heart of winter's decree.

Silent nights, the air so clear,
Sparks of hope that seem so near.
Every breath a vapored glow,
As time within the stillness flows.

Moonlight's touch on blankets white,
Guides the dreams that take to flight.
Through the chill, our spirits soar,
In this realm, we long for more.

The world feels vast, yet so confined,
Lost in thoughts of heart and mind.
Yet winter's chill, a bittersweet,
Unfurled dreams beneath our feet.

As dawn awakens with the sun,
A brighter day has just begun.
In every flake, a story swirled,
A canvas of our frozen world.

Shrouded in White

Veils of snow embrace the earth,
A soft hush upon its girth.
Candles glow in windows bright,
As they share the warmth of light.

Footpaths lost beneath the frost,
In a world where none are lost.
Every tree adorned in grace,
Wearing winter's pure embrace.

Frosty breath floats in the air,
Nature's stillness everywhere.
Time seems paused in this delight,
All is hushed, so pure, and bright.

Twilight dances, shadows blend,
In the silence, hearts transcend.
Wrapped in stillness, soft and tight,
Finding peace in shrouded white.

As the evening sky turns deep,
Winter dreams begin to seep.
In this wonder, pure and right,
We find solace in the night.

Lullabies of the Frozen Night

In the stillness of the night,
Whispers of dreams take flight.
Blankets of snow softly lay,
Hushing the world till break of day.

Stars twinkle in the cold,
Stories of warmth to be told.
Moonlight dances on white fields,
Secrets of winter it yields.

Frosted windows softly glow,
Echoes of a world below.
Sleep now, dear child, so snug,
In winter's deep, tender hug.

Sledding circles wander wide,
In dreams where laughter can't hide.
Each lullaby, a gentle hum,
Of joy and comfort, now come.

So let the snow softly fall,
As night blankets one and all.
Find warmth in the silent snow,
In dreams, let your spirit go.

Echoes of a Snowbound Dream

Whispers of night in the air,
Snowflakes dance without a care.
Each flake tells a story bright,
In the magic of moonlight.

Silent streets wrapped in white,
Softened edges, pure delight.
Footsteps crunch like brittle glass,
Echoes of times that swiftly pass.

Beneath the stars, shadows play,
In the chill of the fading day.
Roots of dreams, deep in the ground,
Where echoes of winter are found.

Hushed charm in the frozen sigh,
As winter blankets the sky.
With each breath, a dream takes flight,
In the canvas of the night.

So let the world turn slow and bright,
In the echoes of a snowbound night.
Find the beauty in the freeze,
As you drift in the winter breeze.

Beneath the Winter's Veil

Softly falls the winter's breath,
Whispers of a world at rest.
Underneath the snowy cloak,
Silent dreams, the heart awoke.

Golden light in the distance gleams,
Awakening the quiet dreams.
Each flake a promise on the ground,
In frosted peace, love is found.

Branches draped like crystal lace,
Nature's beauty, a warm embrace.
In the hush of a silent morn,
New beginnings gently born.

Listen closely to the sound,
Life's sweet secret, all around.
Underneath the softest white,
Magic lingers, pure delight.

So hold these moments, keep them near,
For winter's song is crystal clear.
Beneath the veil, a world unfolds,
In the arms of winter, behold.

The Subtle Language of Frost

Frost paints whispers on the glass,
Each pattern a gentle pass.
Nature speaks in silent tones,
A symphony of ice and bones.

Lurking shadows, soft and shy,
Silent messages in the sky.
Each breath clouding, in the night,
Holds tales of warmth and moonlight.

Winter's breath, a gentle sigh,
As the world slows and dreams fly.
Beneath the surface, heartbeats thrum,
In the quiet, life has come.

Glistening branches sway like dreams,
In the moonlight, they softly gleam.
The language of frost, a soft call,
Reminds us of the warmth in all.

So listen close to the winter's song,
In its silence, you belong.
With every layer of icy gloss,
Find wisdom in the subtle frost.

A Canvas of White Dreams

In the still of a snowy night,
The world wrapped in soft, pure light.
Footprints leave their gentle trace,
Whispers of dreams in this quiet space.

Branches draped in frosty lace,
Silent beauty, a tranquil embrace.
The moon hangs low, a watchful eye,
As winter's breath enchants the sky.

Snowflakes dance in a swirling flight,
Painting the earth, aglow and bright.
Each flake unique, a fleeting sigh,
A moment caught, as time drifts by.

Candles flicker, warm and near,
Casting shadows, drawing cheer.
Hot cocoa in hand, we gather close,
Sharing tales, the ones we cherish most.

In this realm of white and peace,
Unity is found, our hearts release.
A canvas where memories bloom,
Framed by winter's gentle gloom.

Shimmers of the Icy Whisper

Through the pines, whispers weave,
Icy shimmers on the eaves.
The air is crisp, a chilling breath,
Nature wrapped in elegant dress.

Stars twinkle like diamonds bright,
Illuminating the tranquil night.
A gentle breeze sings through the trees,
Carrying secrets upon the breeze.

Footsteps crunch on frosty ground,
Echoes of peace are all around.
In the stillness, a soft retreat,
Where time stands still, our hearts find beat.

Moonlight spills like silver hue,
Painting shadows in the dew.
Softly, the world begins to dream,
In this magic, our spirits gleam.

Each icy whisper tells a tale,
Of winter's beauty, strong and frail.
We wrap ourselves in nature's song,
In this wonder, we all belong.

In the Heart of a Snowstorm

Whirling winds of feathery white,
In the heart of the storm's fierce bite.
Snowflakes spin in a wild dance,
Nature's fury, an icy trance.

Visibility fades, the world obscured,
Yet there's a quietude, so pure.
Trees bow down, heavy with snow,
A majestic sight, a tranquil show.

Homeward bound, the hearth aglow,
As storm winds howl, fierce and low.
We gather close, share tales of old,
In each other's warmth, we find our hold.

The beauty lies in chaos' heart,
Where winter's artistry plays its part.
A fleeting moment, harsh yet fair,
In snowstorms, dreams linger in the air.

Each flake tells a story, unique and bright,
In the heart of winter's toughest flight.
We find our way through winds that roam,
In the heart of a snowstorm, we find home.

Shadows beneath Winter's Quilt

Beneath the quilt of winter's grace,
Shadows weave in a hidden place.
Frosted ground under moon's soft glow,
An enchanting realm where spirits flow.

Silence wraps the world so tight,
Stars shimmer down, a guiding light.
The chill of night begins to creep,
While winter's secrets softly seep.

Trees stand tall in solemn lines,
Guardians of dreams, of ancient signs.
Each branch etched sharp under snow's weight,
Beneath the quilt, we contemplate.

Crackling fires bring warmth and cheer,
As we draw close, those held dear.
In whispers, memories take their flight,
Shadows dance in the still of night.

Through the frost, our hopes ignite,
In the quilted shadows, pure delight.
Winter's breath holds us tight and near,
Together we share this season's cheer.

The Quiet Dance of Flurries

Snowflakes fall with gentle grace,
Whispers soft in winter's embrace.
A silent waltz drapes the ground,
Nature's peace is all around.

Each flurry spins, a fleeting glance,
They twist and turn, a quiet dance.
Through bare trees, they like to play,
In the hush of a silvered day.

Pine trees bow, heavy with white,
Veils of frost hide the night's light.
Footsteps muffled, air so still,
Heartbeats pause on the hill.

Glistening trails beneath moon's gaze,
Lost in this frozen maze.
Night wraps tightly, stars aglow,
In this dance, we feel the flow.

As dawn awakens, shadows fade,
The quiet dance begins to trade.
Yet in our hearts, a memory stays,
Of flurries' waltz on winter's days.

Trace of the Frost's Lull

In whispers cold, the dawn arrives,
With frosty breath, the old earth thrives.
Patterns lace the glassy pane,
A silent verse, serene refrain.

Bare branches wear a diamond crown,
Emerald boughs in winter's gown.
Each frost-kissed leaf, a story told,
Of sleepy nights and dreams of old.

Clouds gather, draped in gray hue,
As time slows down, dreams come true.
A tranquil hush, a fleeting spell,
In the heart, a magic dwells.

The dawn unfolds, mist in its wake,
A world reborn from winter's ache.
With every breath, a sigh of peace,
In frosty grips, we find release.

The trace of frost will melt away,
Yet hearts will hold this cool ballet.
In whispers soft, the memories cling,
Of winter's kiss and the joy it brings.

Hidden Lullabies in Ice

Underneath the quilt of snow,
Nature hums a soft hello.
In glistening light, the secrets lie,
Hidden lullabies whispering nigh.

Icicles hang like notes in air,
Chilling songs of winter's care.
The brook is still, a crystal flow,
In frozen dreams where whispers go.

Each flake a voice, a gentle sigh,
In nature's choir under the sky.
Wrapped in warmth, we pause to hear,
The melodies we hold so dear.

Hushed the world in silver glow,
Every heartbeat starts to slow.
Together we seek that soft embrace,
Where hidden songs find their place.

In the glimmer of a frosty light,
The earth sings low, deep in the night.
A lullaby where time stands still,
In winter's heart, we feel the thrill.

Caress of a Winter's Night

Stars shimmer bright in the velvet sky,
The world wrapped softly, a gentle sigh.
Snow blankets all in a hush so deep,
While the earth below drifts off to sleep.

Moonlight dances across the ground,
In this frozen realm, peace is found.
With every breath, the air is crisp,
In winter's hold, we find our bliss.

Fires crackle, shadows play,
In cozy corners, hearts sway.
Blankets pulled up to chin,
In the warmth, our dreams begin.

The night whispers secrets untold,
Through frosted windows, tales unfold.
Each moment cherished, wrapped in light,
In the caress of a winter's night.

As dawn approaches, shadows wane,
Yet the magic of night remains.
In our hearts, the warmth ignites,
From the caress of winter's nights.

Snowflakes' Soft Serenade

Delicate dancers in the night,
Twirling softly, pure and bright.
A hush of wonder fills the air,
As winter's magic we all share.

Each flake a story, falling free,
Whispers of what it means to be.
In silence, they embrace the ground,
Creating beauty all around.

Gentle, they kiss the sleeping earth,
Bringing joy and tender mirth.
With every swirl, they weave a dream,
In silver light, they softly gleam.

Through darkened nights and coldest days,
They sparkle in a million ways.
A fleeting moment, soon they fade,
Their perfect form, a grand parade.

So let us cherish each cold night,
As snowflakes dance in soft moonlight.
For in their fall, a symphony,
Of nature's love, so wild and free.

The Chill of Stillness

Beneath the moon, a quiet grace,
Winter's breath, a soft embrace.
The world is hushed, as time stands still,
Each glimmering star, a distant thrill.

Frosted whispers upon the trees,
Carry secrets on the breeze.
In every shadow, silence flows,
A tranquil peace that gently grows.

The night unfolds its snowy veil,
With crystal echoes of a tale.
A magical realm, wrapped in white,
Where dreams take flight in the soft night.

Stillness reigns in the frosty air,
A moment paused, beyond compare.
As nature rests, a world asleep,
In winter's arms, the calm runs deep.

So breathe it in, the chilly air,
Embrace the quiet, without a care.
For in this stillness, peace we find,
A gentle balm for heart and mind.

Veiled in Frost

Veiled in frost, the world anew,
A shimmering coat in morning dew.
Nature's canvas, pure and grand,
A silent touch from winter's hand.

Every branch and blade of grass,
Sparkles bright as shadows pass.
In daylight's glow, their beauty sings,
A realm enchanted, where magic clings.

Beneath the chill, life still thrives,
In frozen beauty, the earth survives.
Each moment glistens, soft and clear,
A tale of wonder, drawing near.

The air is crisp, with whispers low,
A timeless dance, a gentle flow.
Veils of white, in sunlight's gleam,
Bring forth the dreamers, who dare to dream.

As daylight fades, twilight descends,
The beauty lingers, never ends.
In frosty whispers, life takes flight,
Veiled in frost, we say goodnight.

Whispers of the Frozen Realm

Whispers echo through the trees,
Carried softly on the breeze.
In a realm where cold winds roam,
The frozen heart finds a home.

Snow-draped paths, a world so white,
Guiding wanderers with pure light.
Each step a story, slow and clear,
Of winter's magic drawing near.

Frosty breath upon the air,
Tales of wonder linger there.
In every flake, a spark divine,
The frozen realm, where stars align.

As night descends with velvet grace,
Silence weaves a warm embrace.
In the stillness, secrets dwell,
Whispers soft, like a gentle bell.

So let us wander, hand in hand,
Through this enchanted, frosty land.
For in each whisper, we will find,
The frozen realm, a love entwined.

In the Embrace of Chill

Crisp air whispers through the trees,
Frosty breath of winter's tease.
Snowflakes swirl in gentle flight,
Blanketing the world in white.

Hidden paths with secrets old,
Stories of the brave and bold.
Silent footsteps, shadows glide,
In this peace, we take our stride.

Cold stars twinkle in the night,
Guiding dreams with silvery light.
Nature's breath, a calm refrain,
In the chill, embrace the gain.

With each chill, our spirits rise,
Finding warmth in winter's sighs.
By the fire, hearts beat strong,
In this season, we belong.

Embrace the quiet, breathe it in,
Feel the cold, let warmth begin.
In every flake, a tale unfolds,
In the chill, our life beholds.

Enchanted by the White Dance

Glistening flakes in moonlight glow,
Whirling soft, a gentle flow.
Each spin a moment, pure delight,
Enchanted by this snowy night.

Branches wear a crystal crown,
In this silence, hearts won't frown.
Magic lingers in the air,
Every breath, a snowy prayer.

Magic carpets drift and twirl,
Nature's wonders, life unfurl.
Whispers of the winter breeze,
Stories told among the trees.

Footprints lead down paths unknown,
In the white dance, love has grown.
Join hands and twirl, hearts afire,
In this moment, we aspire.

Skies of silver, dreams ignite,
In this dance, all feels so right.
With every turn, a world reborn,
In this beauty, hearts adorn.

The Stillness of Twinkling Crystals

Crystals gather on the ground,
Silent beauty all around.
In the stillness, moments freeze,
Whispers echo through the trees.

Morning light begins to glow,
Sparkling gems in sunlit show.
Nature's treasures, pure and bright,
In the stillness, pure delight.

Frozen streams with glimmering grace,
Reflecting worlds, a frozen space.
Memories carved in icy lace,
In their stillness, we find place.

Time stands still, a breath in wait,
Crystalline dreams, we celebrate.
Folded landscapes, white pristine,
In the stillness, all is seen.

Through this calm, our hearts will flow,
In the quiet, love will grow.
The world adorned, a tranquil show,
In the stillness, we will know.

Frosty Murmurs in the Air

Frosty whispers drift and sway,
Carrying tales from far away.
In the air, a story thrives,
Echoes of the chill that thrives.

Breath of winter, soft and clear,
Nurturing dreams that linger near.
Each gust a memory's embrace,
In the frosty air, we trace.

Snowflakes dance, a ballet light,
Painting scenes in colors bright.
Nature's canvas, pure and rare,
Shows us wonders everywhere.

Murmurs sing through quiet nights,
Guiding souls to higher heights.
In the stillness, truth is found,
With each frosty breath, we're bound.

In this moment, hearts do soar,
Timeless whispers we explore.
Frosty murmurs, soft and fair,
In winter's grip, we find our share.

Tales Beneath the Winter Sky

Underneath the starry night,
Whispers of the cold wind bite.
Snowflakes dance in playful glee,
Forgotten tales call out to me.

Fires crackle, stories blend,
Voices echo, winter's friend.
Shadows lengthen, dreams take flight,
In the heart of frosty night.

Moonlight kisses fields of white,
Silent paths shine pure and bright.
Every step, a tale retold,
In the grasp of winter's hold.

Time stands still as dreams ignite,
In the canvas of the night.
Each breath a chill, each sigh a spark,
Woven gently in the dark.

From the past, old stories rise,
Beneath the vast and shimmering skies.
In every flake, a moment traced,
A winter's tale that can't be replaced.

Winter's Gentle Serenade

Softly falls the powder white,
Wrapping all in pure delight.
Winter's song, a tender tune,
Echoes softly 'neath the moon.

In the forest, shadows play,
Swaying branches hide away.
A gentle breeze that twirls and sways,
Whispers of the frosty days.

Crisp air tinged with pine and wood,
Moments cherished, understood.
Fires glow with warmth and cheer,
Carrying tales we hold dear.

Every flake is a note so sweet,
Nature's rhythm, soft and fleet.
Harmonies of silence blend,
Winter's heart, our truest friend.

Nights are long, yet spirits high,
Beneath this vast and starlit sky.
In the still, we find our way,
Winter's song, forever stay.

Traces of the Silver Silence

In the hush of falling snow,
Whispers linger, soft and slow.
Silver blankets hush the ground,
Traces of the peace we've found.

Footprints left in quiet grace,
Nature's touch, a warm embrace.
Silent echoes of the past,
Moments captured, meant to last.

Trees adorned in icy lace,
Guarding secrets time can't face.
In the quiet, memories flow,
Connecting hearts with gentle glow.

Stars alight in velvet sky,
Wishing dreams on high pass by.
In this silver silence, we,
Find our heart's tranquility.

As the world outside stands still,
Time and space begin to fill.
Winter's breath, a subtle guide,
In its embrace, we will abide.

Frostbitten Stories Unfold

Upon the branches, crystals gleam,
Stories held in every beam.
Frostbitten tales of joy and woe,
Carried far on winter's glow.

Each path a mystery to explore,
Echoes of the ones before.
In the stillness, voices blend,
Whispering secrets to a friend.

Time unravels in the freeze,
Moments linger, come with ease.
The chill invites us to confide,
In the warmth that we provide.

Stars above like diamonds shine,
Crafting stories, yours and mine.
In the frost, our dreams take hold,
While sleeping stories are retold.

So let the chill embrace your soul,
As winter's magic makes us whole.
With every breath, a tale begun,
Beneath the watchful, moonlit sun.

Echoes Beneath the Icy Canopy

Whispers glide through frozen trees,
A symphony of silent pleas,
Snowflakes dance, a soft refrain,
Echoes linger in the pain.

Branches bow with icy grace,
Time stands still in this cold space,
Moonlight bathes the world in white,
Drawing shadows into night.

Beneath the frost, a secret song,
Nature's heartbeat, deep and strong,
In the stillness, secrets wait,
Frozen moments, hearts sedate.

Footprints trace a winding way,
Every step, a proud display,
Through the hush, each breath confined,
Lost in echoes, intertwined.

When the dawn breaks, soft and clear,
Warmth will whisper, drawing near,
But beneath the icy dome,
Echoes linger, call me home.

Secret Lullabies of Winter

A blanket white covers the ground,
Softly whispers all around,
Crystals shimmer in the night,
Winter sings, serene and bright.

In the stillness, slumber deep,
Nature hushes, secrets keep,
Dreams entwined in frosty air,
Lullabies, a whispered prayer.

Stars peep through the frigid skies,
Casting light with gentle sighs,
Each twinkle tells a silent tale,
Of soft winds and snowy trails.

As breath forms in misty puffs,
The world unfolds, yet feels so tough,
But in this quiet, hearts will mend,
Winter's song, our faithful friend.

As the dawn begins to break,
Warming hues, the silence shake,
Yet in shadows, peace will stay,
Secret lullabies at play.

Frost-Kissed Dawn

Morning breaks with gentle hue,
Touch of frost on world anew,
Sunrise paints the sky in gold,
Secrets of the night retold.

Icicles glisten, sharp and clear,
Echoes of the night draw near,
Pale sunbeams stretch and yawn,
Embracing every frozen lawn.

Each blade of grass, a crystal shard,
Nature's canvas, bright and hard,
Whispers of the nighttime frost,
Beauty found, though warmth was lost.

The air is crisp, a biting chill,
Yet hearts feel light, a fleeting thrill,
Frost kissed dawn, a fresh embrace,
Time to cherish, time to trace.

In this moment, everything waits,
As sunlight opens autumn gates,
While the world breathes in the morn,
Frost-kissed essence, brightly born.

The Language of Ice

Silent words in a frozen stream,
Nature speaks in quiet dream,
Cracks and lines tell stories bold,
Revealing secrets yet untold.

Frosty whispers fill the air,
A delicate dance, beyond compare,
Each flake a note in winter's score,
The language of ice, forevermore.

In the silence, truths are spun,
Moments caught, each one a pun,
Branches laden with icy lace,
Nature's art, a timeless grace.

As winter wraps the world in white,
Softly seams of day and night,
Wisps of frost, with tales to share,
A language crafted, rare and fair.

Though spring will come and melt away,
Every whisper, every sway,
Will linger still in hearts of those,
Who understand what nature knows.

Hidden Tracks in the Snow

Footprints trace a winding path,
Lost in white and frozen math,
Whispers of a journey bold,
Secrets in the snow unfold.

Branches bow with frosted grace,
Nature holds a quiet space,
Every step a tale to tell,
In the winter's chilly spell.

Distant echoes of the past,
Memories that ever last,
Through the drifts they softly creep,
In the stillness, silence deep.

Beneath the sky, a quiet glow,
Shimmers on the virgin snow,
Each track leads where none have walked,
In this space, the world is shocked.

Hidden tales in every flake,
Whispers of the dreams we make,
As evening descends without a sound,
In the snow, our hearts are found.

Soft Hush of Twilight

Colors blend in gentle sweep,
As day gives way to night's deep keep,
Stars awaken, softly gleam,
In twilight's calm, we softly dream.

Whispers dance on evening's breath,
Calmest time before the death,
Of light that glows, then fades away,
In shadows where the night will play.

The world feels wrapped in velvet hues,
A tranquil stage for night's muse,
Moonlight drapes the hills like lace,
In twilight's warm and sweet embrace.

Crickets sing their lullabies,
Underneath the velvet skies,
With every note, a peace descends,
As time, like water, gently bends.

Here, where dreams and night converge,
Fleeting moments start to surge,
In the softest hush we find,
The beauty of a heart entwined.

The Weight of Solitude

In silent rooms, the shadows move,
Echoes of a heart that groves,
Every breath a heavy sigh,
In the stillness, thoughts run high.

Alone, beneath a starry shroud,
Listening to the silence loud,
Waves of thoughts, a potent tide,
In solitude, we often hide.

Moments stretch like distant shores,
Empty are the open doors,
Yet in the quiet, seeds were sown,
In this space, we find our own.

Fingers trace the lines of grief,
Searching for a kind relief,
Yet in the weight, a strength we find,
In solitude, we've been refined.

Though darkness lingers in its place,
We learn to dance at our own pace,
In every hush, the heart can glean,
The weight of solitude can mean.

Frosty Footprints

In the dawn, a crisp delight,
Frosty footprints, pure and white,
Nature's canvas, fresh and bare,
Tales are written everywhere.

Each step leaves a fleeting mark,
In the field, the world's a park,
Paws and soles in icy dance,
Moments caught in winter's trance.

Glistening under morning beams,
Footprints echo hidden dreams,
Paths that wander, twist, and trace,
In the chilly, open space.

As the sun begins to rise,
Casting light in tender skies,
Every track a story spun,
In the snow, we find our fun.

Frosty footprints left behind,
Memories of the kindred mind,
In nature's grip, we wander free,
In every step, a part of me.

Shivering Silence

In the hush of night, still air,
Whispers linger everywhere.
Snowflakes fall, soft and light,
Painting shadows, pure and white.

Silent echoes dance above,
In this frozen world we love.
Every breath a cloud of frost,
In this beauty, never lost.

Time stands still, a quiet hum,
Nature's song, a gentle drum.
Underneath the stars so bright,
Shivering silence, pure delight.

Footsteps crunch on snow so deep,
In this silence, secrets keep.
Wrapped in warmth, we stand so close,
In the stillness, hearts engrossed.

Winter's grace, a tender touch,
In this moment, we feel much.
Together, lost in midnight's glow,
In shivering silence, love will grow.

A Tapestry of Ice

Crystals weave a frosty thread,
Across the ground, where dreams are bred.
Each flake a story, pure and bright,
In the tapestry, a beautiful sight.

Fractals dance in moonlit sway,
Crafting magic in disarray.
Glistening paths, they beckon near,
Whispering secrets for us to hear.

Winter's breath so cold and clear,
Holds the beauty we hold dear.
In the silence of the night,
Nature's canvas, pure delight.

Wonders weave with icy grace,
Every corner, a new embrace.
Underneath the starlit dome,
In the tapestry, we find home.

Frozen moments caught in time,
Echoing life's forgotten rhyme.
A world adorned with endless white,
A reminder of pure, sweet light.

Gentle Crystals Falling

Falling softly, gems of snow,
Glistening softly in the glow.
Whispers carried on the breeze,
Dancing lightly through the trees.

Each flake unique, a work of art,
Cradled gently, touched by heart.
Floating down with such grace,
Transforming this familiar place.

Under blankets, soft and white,
Winter wraps the world in light.
Every inch, a silent spell,
In this wonder, all is well.

Crystals twirl, a ballet grand,
Adorning earth, a diamond band.
In the twilight, shadows play,
As night transforms the light of day.

Closing eyes, I breathe it in,
Gentle crystals, where dreams begin.
Snowflakes fall and softly gleam,
A winter's blessing, pure as a dream.

The Softest of Covers

Snowfall drapes the world in white,
A gentle hush envelops night.
Softest of covers, pure and neat,
Blanketing dreams with silent feet.

Laughter echoes, children play,
In the magic of winter's sway.
Creating angels, joy revealed,
In the softness, hearts are healed.

With each breath, the air is cold,
In this wonder, stories told.
Underneath the stars' embrace,
The softest of covers claims its space.

Quiet moments, peaceful scenes,
Whispers trace through silvered dreams.
Wrapped in warmth, together we sigh,
As the world twinkles, a lullaby.

Winter nights hold promise dear,
In the silence, love draws near.
Soft covers hide the world below,
In this beauty, forever flow.

Whispers in Ice

In the stillness, secrets lie,
Frozen murmurs, soft and shy.
Chill of night, a gentle sigh,
Echoes of the stars up high.

Crystal chains, the branches bear,
Silent dreams, hang in the air.
Nature's quilt, a silver stare,
Whispers of winter, oh so rare.

Underneath the moonlit glow,
Footsteps crunching in the snow.
Cold winds wrap like softest woe,
A quiet dance, the heartbeats flow.

Glistening frost, the world adorned,
A fleeting touch, so sweet, so scorned.
In this realm, the senses mourned,
Fading warmth, the light has torn.

Yet in shadows, hope does bloom,
Spring awaits beyond the gloom.
With every sigh the chill will loom,
But life will rise to chase the doom.

Hushed Blossoms of Winter

Petals whisper in the breeze,
Soft and still, as time can freeze.
Frosted dreams on silent trees,
Winter's breath, a gentle tease.

Colors muted, shades of white,
Nature wraps in soft delight.
Beneath the stars, a tranquil night,
Hushed blossoms tremble in the light.

Silent gardens, wrapped in snow,
In stillness, life begins to grow.
Hidden beauty in the glow,
Winter's charm, a soft tableau.

From the ground, the buds arise,
Cloaked in frost beneath the skies.
Nature's magic in disguise,
Winter's heart that never dies.

So let the world in quiet rest,
Where blooms lie hidden, gently pressed.
In winter's warmth, they are blessed,
Hushed whispers of a silent quest.

A Veil of Winter's Breath

Glistening flakes of powdered white,
Covering ground, a pure delight.
Each breath hangs, a frosted sight,
A veil of calm, the world ignites.

Shadows dance in silver light,
Softly glows the stars at night.
In cold embrace, the whispers bite,
Winter's breath, a sweet invite.

Frozen rivers, softly flowing,
Through the woods, excitement growing.
In the stillness, secrets showing,
Hushed together, time is slowing.

Through the pines, a gentle rustle,
Nature's hymn, a soft tussle.
Traces left where snowflakes hustle,
Winter's breath, a cozy bustle.

In the hush, we find our peace,
As frozen moments never cease.
Life may pause but never fleece,
In winter's way, the heart finds lease.

Tranquil Snowfall

Snowflakes fall, a soft embrace,
Blanketing the world in grace.
Whispers sweet, in silent space,
Tranquil dreams begin to trace.

Gentle dances, soft and light,
Covering the earth so white.
In the stillness, hearts take flight,
Finding joy in winter's night.

Crystals twinkle, stars in flight,
Beneath the moon, a guiding sight.
In the cold, the world feels bright,
Wrapped in warmth, a soft delight.

Hushed reflections, thoughts unfurl,
While shadows curl, the snow does twirl.
In frozen breaths, emotions whirl,
Woven dreams of winter's pearl.

Through the night, the beauty stays,
In quiet peace, our spirit plays.
With every flake, the heart obeys,
Tranquil snowfall, timeless ways.

Echoes of the Frozen Wind

Whispers dance on icy breath,
Through the trees they weave and sway.
Nature's voice, a chilling thread,
Echoes of the night and day.

Shadows fall where silence sleeps,
In the dark, the secrets keep.
Footsteps muffled, gently tread,
Leaving marks, then fade ahead.

Snowflakes spiral, twinkling bright,
Each a gem in moon's soft light.
Carried far on winter's breeze,
Tales of heart, lost memories.

As the cold wraps all around,
In the hush, a hopeful sound.
Promises in frost are made,
In the chill, our dreams displayed.

When the dawn breaks, warmth will rise,
Melting all beneath clear skies.
But in twilight's tender kiss,
Echoes linger, sweet abyss.

The Sound of Winter's Caress

Softly falls the gentle snow,
Nature's blanket, pure and white.
Whispers of the wind, they flow,
Through the stillness of the night.

Trees adorned in sparkling lace,
Stand like sentries, poised and proud.
Time moves slow in this calm space,
Wrapped in silence, soft and shroud.

Footfalls crunch on frozen ground,
Each step echoes like a song.
In this peace, our hearts are found,
Winter's embrace, warm and strong.

Stars peek through the frosted veil,
Twinkling bright, a distant dance.
In this moment, love prevails,
Magic whispers, take a chance.

Soon the thaw will melt away,
Yet these moments stay in mind.
In our hearts, they softly play,
Winter's touch, forever kind.

A Shroud of Solitude

In the stillness, shadows creep,
Wrapped in cold, the world is hushed.
Time stands still as secrets keep,
Beneath a cloak of white, we're brushed.

Lonely echoes drift and sway,
Through the branches, bare and stark.
In this silence, hearts display,
Whispers lost within the dark.

Snowy blankets hide the pain,
Covering the scars once bare.
Yet the beauty, not in vain,
Hides the heart's deep, quiet prayer.

As the frost holds tight its reign,
Dreams of warmth begin to swell.
In this shroud, there's growth, not bane,
Life prepares its tale to tell.

Though solitude may try to bind,
A spark of hope breaks through the chill.
In the quiet, love will find,
Pathways strong, our hearts to fill.

Silent Frost

Underneath the silver moon,
Frosted whispers softly sing.
In this hour, the cold blooms soon,
Winter's breath, a gentle ring.

Branches glisten, diamonds bright,
Caught in moments, time stood still.
In the cloak of endless night,
Every heartbeat, every thrill.

Footsteps light on frozen trails,
Carved in snow, a map of dreams.
Where the wind tells hidden tales,
And the world is not what seems.

Chill that wraps around the heart,
Biding time, a longing's call.
In this quiet, we won't part,
For in silence, we find all.

Days may pass, the thaw will creep,
Yet memories will hold the frost.
In our souls, this silence keep,
In the stillness, we are lost.